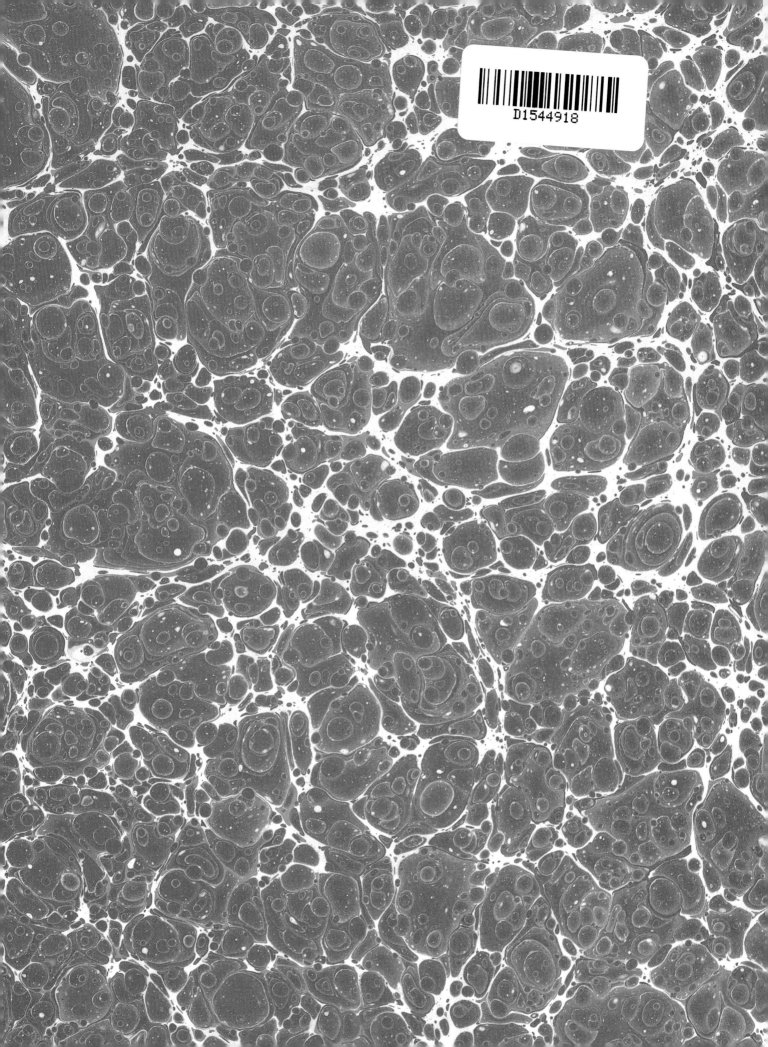

THE CAPE COD HOUSE

AMERICA'S MOST POPULAR HOME

by Stanley Schuler

West Chester, Pennsylvania 19380

Printed in the United States of America.
Library of Congress Catalog Number: 82-80857.
ISBN: 0-916838-63-3
This book may be purchased from the publisher.
Please include $2.00 postage.
Try your bookstore first.

Published by Schiffer Publishing Ltd.
1469 Morstein Road, West Chester, Pennsylvania 19380
Write for free catalog.

PREFACE

To the best of my knowledge, all the Cape Cod houses pictured in *The Cape Cod House* are still standing. Unfortunately, only four of them are open to the public on a fairly regular basis but you can see the others from the outside as you drive the country's roads and byways.

A great many of the earliest houses bear the owner's name. During my picture-taking expeditions, however, I discovered (1) that the name assigned to a house is not always that of the original owner, as I think it should be, and (2) that even in small towns the residents are usually unable to direct you to a house when you give them only the early owner's name. So I have omitted all names except those of a handful of the most famous Capes.

I wish that I could include plans of all the houses but for one reason or another many are not available. In the case of the old houses, even the plans shown are not necessarily faithful to the houses as they were built. Capes, like other ancient houses, have changed considerably over the years. So the old plans I have included are simply educated guesses.

Many people have helped me with this book. Special thanks are due George Tatum, eminent architectural historian; William Ward, architect and student of early America; Paul J. White, who lives on the Cape, studying and saving old houses; Richard Beatty, creator and editor of Colonial Homes; Richard Wills, for letting me use pictures that appeared in the books his firm has published; my daughter Miranda Burnett; and my sister-in-law Margaret Schuler.

Stanley Schuler

THE CAPE COD HOUSE

Timothy Dwight, president of Yale, toured Cape Cod in 1800 and he is generally credited with giving the Cape Cod house its name. He observed in his "Travels in New England and New York" that the small, one-and-a-half-story homes that dotted the Cape from its narrow neck at Bourne to Provincetown were so much of a pattern that they constituted a "class which may be called, with propriety, Cape Cod houses".

There is no evidence, however, that the Cape Cod house—or Cape Cod cottage—actually originated on the Cape. Or that it did not. The earliest house still standing on that long, arm-shaped neck of land—the Saconesset Homestead at West Falmouth—is presumed to have been built in 1678.[1] But in Old Lyme, Connecticut, roughly 100 miles westward, the William Peck house and another unnamed house are dated 1666.

Furthermore, Hingham, Massachusetts—just south of Boston—today has as many if not more ancient Cape Cod houses per square mile than the entire Cape ever boasted. So Mr. Dwight might better have called the Cape Cod house the Hingham house or the Lyme/Old Lyme house (after another area with innumerable Capes) or something else.

But it has come down through time as the Cape Cod house, and by this name it will always be known—with affection and admiration.

It is distinctively American despite its English origins.

It is lovely. Royal Barry Wills once wrote: "A glimpse of a wide doorway, of white clapboards in the sun, of bittersweet in the garden—such are the houses of Cape Cod. They line the quiet, shady streets of the villages—as unpretentious as they are livable. Carping critics may poke fun at their rambler roses, picket fences and stately elms, but such things spell home to most of us."

It is practical and economical.

It has been and, if a precise count could be taken, may still be the most popular, most common style of house in the United States.

Yet it has been ignored, totally or virtually, by almost all eminent architectural historians. And we know remarkably little about its actual development because it was the product of a people rather than an individual; because few if any of the very earliest houses still stand;[2] and because only fragmentary written or pictorial

---

[1] This does not mean that there were not earlier houses that have disappeared. But for whatever they are worth, all official documents recording them were destroyed when the Barnstable County Courthouse burned to the ground in the early 1800s.

[2] The dates proudly displayed on ancient houses must be taken with a grain of salt. Many spring from the imagination of an owner or local historian with chamber-of-commerce inclinations. Many more can be attributed to the common practice of reading into a town's legal documents more than is actually there. For example, Old Lyme land records show that William Peck bought the land on which his house stands in 1666; but this does not mean that he built at that time or that the house now standing is the original house. "Positive" dating of very early building can be established only by a date carved into the original framing; and even this might be suspect because the framing member could have been salvaged from an earlier house. Approximate dating can often be established by close examination of the house by an architectural historian skilled in such matters. But here again there is considerable chance of error. I inspected the Peck house with one of the country's foremost experts on early architecture, but it has been so altered and covered over that even he could say only that it is a very early structure.

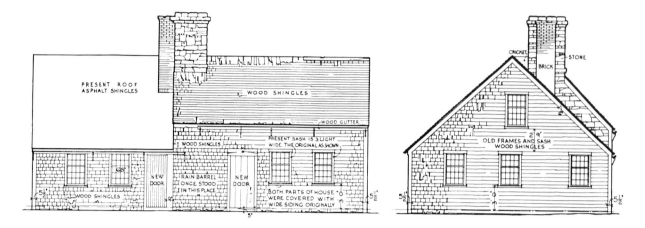

Waite-Potter house. The 1677 house was the right-hand section. The smaller part was added. HABS drawing.

descriptions have survived—if they were ever put on paper at all.

For a long time after the Pilgrims settled Plymouth they lived in huts little better than children today build in backyards. It was not until about 1630, when the colony was firmly established, that respectable permanent dwellings began to rise.

The Pilgrims were simple people, not very creative or imaginative, and quite logically, the homes they put up were much like those they had left in England and, to lesser extent, Holland: small rectangles, one story high, with steep gable roofs covered with thatch or sometimes hand-split pine shingles. Almost exactly at ground level was a single room with a huge fireplace at one end. Here the entire family lived and slept. Under the roof was a loft reached by a ladder and wide open to the first floor. This was used, if necessary, as overflow sleeping space but mainly it held the casks of dried fish, vegetables and other foods put up for the winter. Windows were few and tiny, glazed with oiled parchment or cloth or left completely open except for inside shutters that were slid across them. The lone exterior door, though stoutly constructed to keep out Indians, did not fit tightly in the low doorway. Despite the fire kept burning in the fireplace, the house was cold, dark, smoky and smelly.

The houses on display today at Plimouth Plantation are good facsimiles of the colonists' homes (none of which is left). By the Plantation's own admission, they are probably not totally accurate reproductions but it was from something very much like them that the Cape Cod house evolved.

How fast it evolved is anyone's guess. If the William Peck house was indeed built in 1666 and the Saconesset Homestead in 1678, the process was quite rapid (when you consider that home building, although of utmost importance, was just one of many things the busy, harassed colonists had to think about). It seems equally likely that the evolution was more gradual, because the original part of the Waite-Potter house, which was built in 1677 in South Westport, Massachusetts, is a transitional design. Like the Plymouth houses, it has a single room and loft and a large end fireplace. But the roof pitch has been reduced and the windows enlarged approximately to Cape Cod standards.

In view of its English/Plymouth antecedents, it is fair to assume that the first true Cape Cod house was of roughly the same size and basic plan as the Waite-Potter house. But the Peck and Saconesset houses indicate it was not. These are more than three times larger; look almost exactly like the Cape that most

6

of us instantly visualize when Cape Cod houses are mentioned. Here, then, is another mystery.

The early Cape Cod house has characteristics that mark it clearly for what it is. Nevertheless, there are a good many early Southern houses and even some Middle-Atlantic-state houses that can be confused with it.

The Cape Cod house forms a compact rectangle. (Even though additions have been made to most houses, the original structure usually stands out boldly.)

It sits very close to the ground and generally faces south.

It has an unbroken gable roof pitched steeply enough to provide living space with headroom underneath. The facade is approximately 8 feet high. From sills to roof peak, the house measures approximately 20 feet.

It has a massive chimney that rises through the roof ridge and is, in the large houses, centrally located between the gable ends.

It is of frame construction. The walls are clad with wood shingles or clapboards.[3] The roof is wood-shingled.

The rather small, multi-paned windows[4] and doorway are placed close under the eaves.

The eaves and rakes project only a few inches beyond the walls.

There are as many as five windows of several sizes in the gables to light the second floor.

Exterior ornamentation is totally lacking.

On the first floor are three main rooms, each heated by its own fireplace. The second floor, or garret, was complete-ly open in the beginning but has since been partitioned off in various ways.

Over-all, the early Cape Cod house is an extremely simple, self-effacing, almost austere structure. Yet it is so well proportioned that it is beautiful in any setting. And it was perfectly adapted to its occupants — which is more than most architectural styles can claim.

How it turned out as it did is purely conjecture.

Assuming that the Cape Cod house originated on the Cape, other writers have emphasized the idea that the house is the product of its environment. As New England goes, Cape Cod does not have a particularly hostile climate. It is cooler in summer and warmer in winter than inland areas. It has little snow. But it is exposed as no other area is exposed to wind — howling, roaring, salt-spray-laden winds that bend the trees, move the sand and played a major part in stripping the land of the "excellent black earth to a spit's depth" that the Pilgrims extolled. These winds unquestionably shaped the early houses on the Cape. And while the wind is less persistently menacing in other shoreline New England areas, it can be severe enough to have shaped the similar houses built there.

The wind, in other words, explains why the Cape Cod house was set so close to the ground and had minimum vertical surfaces, a relatively low-pitched roof and virtually no projections: It could ride out storms that would have flattened the taller, more steeply roofed house before it.

The usual, but by no means invariable, orientation of the Cape Cod house to the south, its small windows and large fireplaces were also an obvious response to the environment. They helped to keep the house tolerably warm despite loose construction and lack of insulation.

But the Cape Cod house was much more a product of the people that built it.

Whether they lived on the Cape or in

---

[3] & [4] Clapboards, first made of oak and later of white pine, probably preceded shingles. The first windows were casements, although their construction is unknown. Leaded casements with diamond-shaped panes were in use in 1650 but generally only in the finest houses. It's hard to imagine them in humble Capes. Sash of the double-hung type (except that the upper sash was fixed) did not appear until the early 1700s, but they were then used exclusively in Capes.

Hingham, Lakeville, Old Lyme or Clinton, these were country people. They were not Boston merchants, Salem ship owners, or New Haven bankers.

They had to struggle to make a modest living; therefore their homes were inevitably small and economical. They could not afford to pay much more than the $100 to $200 that a Cape Cod house cost in the 1700s.

They were an isolated people. Of course they came in contact with peddlers, preachers, itinerant craftsmen, families moving across the country; but they saw little of such people so they were slow to catch up with exciting new ideas about architecture, among other things. This was especially true of those living on Cape Cod. Until it became a vacation mecca only a few decades ago, the Cape was always a backwater. The King's Highway (now Route 6A) from the "mainland" was not good enough to allow daily stages to and from Provincetown until 1846. The railroad did not reach Provincetown until 1873. I can remember that, even in 1920, the roads from Mattapoisett to Brewster — a distance of only 50 miles — were so bad, in places nothing but sand, that it took my family the better part of half a day to motor from point to point.

Owners of Cape Cod houses were unpretentious people who, even if they could afford it, did not try to outshine their neighbors. They depended on their neighbors as the neighbors depended on them, and that required keeping things on an even keel, avoiding ostentation. They were well aware that at any moment a disaster might strike their family and they might be reduced to poverty without their neighbors' freely given support.

Thus they were also a unified people and unity tends to foster conformity. This conformity was further strengthened by an ingrained suspicion of the occasional outsider who appeared with bright new ways of doing things.

They were a people governed by the discipline of a harsh church. This demanded modesty in everything they did, including—inferentially—the design and construction of their homes.

They were a people of tightly knit families to which each member was expected to make some contribution. They did everything together; consequently, even if income had not been a contributing factor, they would undoubtedly have built small, compact houses in response to and furtherance of this togetherness.

Finally, the struggle to make a life in a new world had turned them into an efficient, thrifty people that naturally built homes as efficient and thrifty as their boats and ships.

Old Cape Cod houses are found everywhere on the Cape but the great majority are concentrated on the Bay side because the settlers were not foolish enough to try coping with the winds, storms and occasional hurricanes that blast the ocean side. As you travel Route 6A from the Cape Cod Canal to Orleans, where the road joins U.S. Route 6, you see Cape Cod houses of every vintage on both sides. And while you are struck by their similarity, you are quickly aware that there are three basic types. According to an early Truro historian, these were designated the "double house", "house and a half", and "house".

The just plain "house" is obviously the direct descendant of the early English/Plymouth house. As noted earlier, logic holds that this must have been the first true Cape Cod house; and the fact that it was called simply a "house" supports this belief. Nevertheless, no definite evidence has been uncovered to prove that the three types were not born more or less simultaneously. Down through the years they developed and flourished together.

Modern terminology for the three house types is different. The double house is now called a "full Cape"; the house and a half is a "three quarter Cape"; the house is

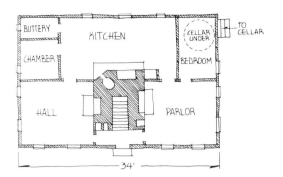

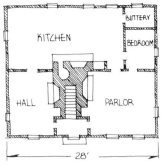

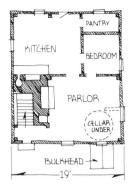

Full Cape   Three-quarter Cape   Half Cape

a "half Cape". And there are also a quarter Cape" and a "double Cape" (modern parlance for two full Capes joined end to end;, but these are so rare that they cannot be considered basic types.

The full Cape is to modern Americans everywhere the standard Cape Cod house, although in earliest days it was probably the least prevalent type because it was the largest. It is roughly 34 to 40 feet long and 28 feet wide. The chimney is precisely centered on the roof above the front door. The door is flanked on both sides by a pair of windows equally spaced. Viewed head on, the picture is one of perfect balance.

In the three-quarter Cape, which is about 28 feet long, the door is slightly off-center and flanked on one side by two windows, on the other side by one. The chimney is centered above the door.

In the half Cape—about 20 feet long—the door is at one end of the house and there are two windows between it and the other end of the house. Here, too, the chimney is normally centered above the door—which means that, depending on the chimney's size, it is set in from the end of the roof a foot or more and is entirely concealed within the house. In this respect the house differs from the Waite-Potter and early Plymouth houses in which the chimney was flush with the end of the roof and formed the end wall of the house. (It is also quite different from Cape-Cod-like

southern houses, in which the chimney projects beyond the end wall.)

In the quarter Cape, which is still smaller, the facade is pierced by only a single window and a door. In the only example that I am familiar with, the chimney is at the window end of the house.

The floor plans of the full, three-quarter and half Capes are not so standardized as some people think. True, they have an essential sameness: An experienced burglar would not run into many surprises as he groped his way through a dark house. But no home owner was afraid to deviate from the standard plan if he thought it would produce a dwelling more suited to his family's needs.

In one way, however, the full Capes are almost always alike: When you open the front door, you step into a small entry that is somewhat wider than deep. Ahead of you, though hidden, is the huge fireplace/chimney block, which anchors the house against the gales. To either side of the entry are virtually identical, more or less square rooms, each with its own roughly 3 x 3-foot fireplace, each with two front and one side windows. These were known as the parlor and hall, best room and lodging room, or east and great rooms. The parlor—with the best furniture, including a bed—was used for funerals, weddings, visits by the minister and other important folk. The hall was a

9

multi-purpose room serving as the master bedroom, a family gathering room and probably a work room.[5]

In the back of the house was the kitchen, or keeping room. It was variously dimensioned, because it was in this part of the house that the owners mainly expressed their personal preferences; but as a rule it is an oblong room, often quite narrow. Here the family lived, soaking up or suffering from the heat from the mammoth fireplace with its beehive oven. Here they cooked, ate, made furniture and worked at everything else under the sun, did whatever close knit families did together. An outside door at the back or side led to the well, privy, other buildings and garden.

At one or both ends of the kitchen were several small rooms. One of these was the buttery (pronounced "buttry" and often spelled that way) used for storage of food, dishes and whatever, for separating milk and churning butter, and also for food preparation. The other was a bedroom. This was the only room in the house called a bedroom; any other rooms used more or less solely for sleeping were chambers. Today this little room has been renamed the borning room, because, besides housing the sick and infirm, it was here that new babies were delivered and nurtured, out of the way but close to their hard-working mothers. It was placed in the kitchen area so it could be kept warm by the ever-burning fire. To the same end, it had only one window; and in a few houses windows were omitted entirely on the theory that light was harmful to infant eyes.

In addition to these two standard rooms, there were frequently one or two extra small chambers.

Ceilings throughout the first floor were only 7 feet high.

Below the buttery, or perhaps the

borning room, was a cellar for winter storage of vegetables and summer storage of perishables. Walled with a single tier of special, somewhat wedge-shaped bricks, it was circular to withstand the pressure of the surrounding soil and less than 12 feet across.

The second floor was reached by a stairway that was frequently about as steep as a ship's companionway. This sometimes went up from the kitchen, in which case it was customarily sealed off by a wall and door to prevent heat loss from the kitchen. In other cases, it almost literally climbed up the steeply sloped outside walls of the fireplaces to where they met at the base of the chimney. Several arrangements are illustrated. The most beguiling—and somehow the most incongruous for such simple houses—came to be known as Good Morning stairs. When you step through the front door, they are dead ahead, practically within arm's reach. A flight of six or seven steps goes straight up to a tiny landing. From both sides of the landing a couple more steps rise to the second floor. The romantic name attached to the scheme is supposed to stem from the fact that, as the family members who slept upstairs arose and raced to the warmth of the kitchen, they met on opposite sides of the landing and greeted each other with a cheery "Good morning."

The three-quarter Cape is nothing more than a shortened full Cape. The parlor is the same size but the hall is much narrower. Similarly, space is squeezed out of the kitchen and its related rooms.

In the half Cape only the parlor remains at the front of the house, although occasional home owners managed to work a tiny chamber in behind the front entry and parlor fireplace. At the back of the house, diagonally opposite the parlor so its large fireplace could share the chimney with the parlor fireplace was the kitchen, or hall. Behind the parlor, at the end of the kitchen, were the borning room and buttery. The stairs to the second floor rose

---

[5] In half houses, the hall often contained a bed but was used primarily as the kitchen. It was also known as the keeping room or fire room.

from the entry or kitchen between the fireplace block and the end wall of the house.

It is anyone's guess why our ancestors built half houses. They left no explanation. Was it for lack of money? Was it because what was good enough for their forebears was good enough for them? Were the houses built by young couples with the idea of adding on another half house when they were established? Were they built by parents for an unattractive daughter to use as bait to snare a husband? Perhaps all these are answers, and there probably are more.

What we do know is that some half houses as well as bigger Capes were enlarged by lengthening. But generally living space was increased by adding on to the back of the house at one of the corners. First came a rather narrow ell placed behind the buttery so it did not eliminate a kitchen window. This was frequently used as a summer kitchen. Then as time went on additions were made to the ell until they stretched all the way to the barn. Consequently, when you approach an old Cape Cod house head on you have no idea whether it is a small house or has grown into a very sizable structure.

Early Cape Cod houses have also been —and still are—reduced in size and moved. Reductions were made by a process known on the Cape as "flaking"—dismantling part of a house and reassembling the pieces elsewhere. But this was a fairly uncommon practice.

On the other hand, moving Capes was —and is—easy. They were simply placed on rollers and hauled across the countryside—often for great distances. They were also floated across the ocean from Nantucket, across Cape Cod Bay, across the innumerable ponds and inlets on the Cape often for great distances. They were also floated across the ocean from Nantucket[6],

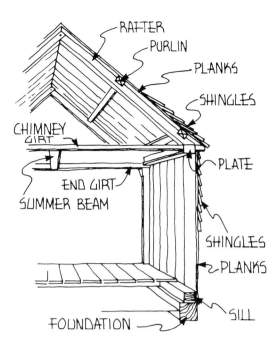

Post and beam framing of early Cape Cod houses.

across Cape Cod Bay, across the innumerable ponds and inlets on the Cape.

Two things in addition to their size made Cape Cod houses—and especially the earliest houses built on Cape Cod—so mobile: They were low-slung, with minimum underpinnings. And they were extremely sturdy.

North and west of Cape Cod, the houses—like other house styles—were built on stone or brick foundations. But Cape Cod is an enormous sandbar with virtually no stones and materials for brickmaking are not of the best (although there were brickyards). So the earliest Capes—a great many of them at least—were underpinned by huge oak timbers supported on piles or rocks. And in a few cases the timbers may have been laid directly on the sand. Thus the owners needed expensive bricks and scarce stones only for fireplaces, chimneys and cellars.

If we today consider this a shoddy

_____

[6] It's generally assumed that the houses moved from Nantucket to the Cape were existing houses, and perhaps some

were. However, Cape Cod houses were not widely built on the island. So it is possible that, when the Nantucket economy faltered, carpenters there built new Cape Cod houses and floated them to the Cape, where they were sold.

method of building—no matter how practical—we cannot say that Cape Cod houses were shoddily constructed in any other way. Indeed, the shoe is on the other foot. The post and beam framing employed by all New England settlers (and their British forebears) was made to last. It was assembled with massive hewn oak timbers joined, not by nails, but by beautiful, intricate wood joints secured with stout oak pegs.

Framing for the front and back walls of a house consisted of the sills supporting the vertical posts, which were placed at the corners and to either side of the front door. Plates were laid across the tops of the posts. Both wall sections were put together on the ground and tilted upright into place. They were then tied together by end girts and one or two chimney girts that ran across the house on either side of the fireplace-chimney block.

The second floor was supported on thick joists spaced about 2 feet apart. These were laid perpendicular to the girts. But if the span between an end girt and chimney girt was too great, a giant summer beam[7] was installed and the joists were then laid between the summer and plates. In either case, the joists were mortised into the large timbers to form a flush surface for the floor. Since the floor served as the first-floor ceiling, joists, summers, girts and plates were exposed.

The roof was formed with large rafters — four on each side — secured to the plates above the posts. Notched-in horizontal purlins tied them together. There were no collar beams or ridge board.

Both the walls and the roof were sheathed with vertical boards 12 to 18 inches wide and at least 1¼ inches thick. This is known as plank-frame construct-

ion.[8] The roof boards were sometimes edge-rabbeted to make tighter joints that supposedly helped to shed rain.

Pine shingles — later, cedar shingles — were used for siding. Some houses were clapboarded on the front and very occasionally on the sides, but clapboarding all four walls was considered ostentatious. It also made for extra expense, for while shingles could be left to weather to a lovely grey, clapboards were painted to prevent the splitting and rapid decay caused by water soaking into the horizontal grain.

On the roof, the shingles — 18 inches long — were so closely lapped that five or six layers of wood covered every point. This may seem to have been an extravagant precaution against leakage, but evidently the builders had reason not to trust shingles any more than the earlier thatch: Since the shingles were hand-split, they did not lie as flat and tight as sawn shingles; and waterproof building paper to lay over the sheathing was unknown.

This great thickness of wood on the roof and walls was the only insulation in the earliest houses, because rough plaster made of pulverized shells and sand or pine paneling was applied directly to the back of the sheathing. This meant that the exterior walls were only about 3 inches thick (as compared with today's 5½ inches); consequently, if the window frames were to be installed flush with the inner wall surfaces, they had to project an inch or so beyond the shingles or clapboards.[9] They did not have casings. In somewhat later houses, however, a thin layer of seaweed was placed in the walls for insulation, and the window frames were pushed back from their projecting positions and trimmed with boards.

---

[7] The "summer" in summer beam is derived either from the French word for "beast of burden"—*sommier*—or from the Latin word for "principal"—*summus.* This beam was the heaviest timber in the frame. It was shaped with a broad axe and the lengthwise corner edges were always chamfered. Sometimes the chamfer was rather elaborately carved. A summer beam with square edges is almost certainly a replacement for an original timber.

---

[8] Plank-frame construction was the primary building method in early Plymouth but did not have its roots in England, where it was rarely employed. The early colonists evidently picked it up during their long stay in Holland, where houses were frequently covered with vertical planks.

[9] The thinness of the walls also explains why the posts were exposed inside the house.

Windows are not a good key to the age of Cape Cod houses because practically all the original sash and frames in the earliest structures rotted out even though they—as well as the siding and exterior doors—may have been treated with fish oil, an early preservative. When they were replaced, it was often with larger sash with thinner muntins (the first were quite heavy, with the glass set very close to the outer edges). This being so, we cannot be certain how the earliers double-hung windows were glazed.[10] It is generally assumed, however, that they had nine 6 by 8 inch rectangular lights in the upper sash, which did not slide, and six in the lower sash. Or frequently they had six over nine lights, twelve over eight or eight over twelve.

Widespread use of blinds did not come along until the late Eighteenth Century. If early houses had them, they were of board and batten construction because the louvered blinds now hanging on the roughly one out of every two houses that are shuttered were a late development. An occasional house did, however, have inside shutters to reduce heat loss.

The placement of windows in the gables often seems eccentric. Henry Thoreau wrote that "the great number of windows in the ends of the houses and their irregularity in size and position struck us agreeably — as if each of the various occupants had punched a hole where his necessities required it and according to his size and stature, without regard to outside effect." Actually, the effect is pleasant. Typically, two large windows in the middle of a gable are flanked by two very small windows and a fifth very small window at the peak for ventilation. But many houses have anywhere from one to four windows. And in some cases the tiny windows are triangular.

[10] The fact that some of the windows seen today have old wavy, amber or violet-tinted glass, called Newcastle glass, does not prove window age. Flawless glass was not produced until quite recently. Furthermore, window glass in early days was costly because it was imported from England and window frames were carpenter-constructed; so old panes were salvaged from rotted-out sash and reused in new sash.

Doorways are more indicative of age although most of the original doors — simple board doors often with an outer vertical layer and inner horizontal layer — are gone with the windows. Many of the early doorways incorporated a transom with four or five small fixed lights. The casings, like the window casings, were plain flat boards; and like the window frames, the door frames were placed directly beneath the plates. But later, when the height of the front and rear walls was increased to give more interior headroom, fanlights were installed over the doors; and still later a few sidelights appeared.

Because doors fitted loosely in the frames, an ingenious way to dispose of the rain that drove in under them was used in some houses. A wide board, either rounded or triangular, was extended into the hall from the sill. This was grooved or ridged along the back edges and the water, collecting in the trough thus formed, was channeled to one or two holes through which it dripped onto the sand below.

The most distinctive feature of the Cape Cod house is the roof.

The gable roof is standard, although its pitch ranges from 8 to 12 inches per horizontal foot. Ten inches is probably average. Few other house styles have such large, steep roofs. No other roof except a gambrel on a one-story Dutch Colonial house or a Mansard so dominates the entire structure. This was especially true in the town of Dennis, where Thoreau found many of the roofs painted red in contrast with the weathered walls.

But the bowed, or rainbow, roof is unique to Cape Cod houses. It is not common; nevertheless, it is more prevalent than appears because the arch of each of the opposing roof surfaces may be so slight that it is discernible only on close examination.

Theoretically, the roof was a product of the shipwrights who settled in the new world. This may well be. Even so, it was not an original idea with them because earlier houses in England had bowed roofs. Their reason for being is unclear. It's difficult to argue that the bow was designed to increase headroom in the attic because even houses with a pronounced bow gained a maximum of only about 12 inches. It seems more likely that the bow was meant simply to strengthen the roof — make it more resistant to compression. Whatever the aim, the home owners who chose the design were obviously in no hurry to move into their new abodes because the shaping of the big rafters took time. Green timbers were laid over a rock and weighted down at the ends until the desired curve was formed and the wood had seasoned.

A few houses in Massachusetts (notably on Cape Ann) and many in Connecticut have gambrel roofs. The earliest is dated 1690. Some authorities maintain that such houses cannot be categorized as Capes, perhaps because they mistakenly believe the gambrel was peculiar to the Dutch (it also appeared in England in about the same period); but in all other respects, the houses are true Capes. However, the roofs do vary. On and near Cape Cod they look as if someone stood beneath each half of a gable roof and gave it a mighty whack that fractured it and pushed it slightly upward. In Connecticut, the lower roof plane rises at a much more acute angle and is pierced by two or three dormer windows. But these are simply regional variations, of which the gambrel roof has many. The primary purpose in all cases was to make the second stories of the houses more livable for adults as well as children. Secondarily, a gambrel roof required short—therefore more readily available—timbers than a gable roof.

Massive chimneys and multiple fireplaces were common, but not peculiar, to Cape Cod houses from the Seventeenth Century to about the fourth decade of the Nineteenth Century. Then stoves began to replace fireplaces and houses built after that time generally have much smaller chimneys that detract from their original solid beauty. Many houses have two small chimneys. However, the switch to stoves did not invariably bring about this unhappy exterior change because some owners ran the flues from stoves placed near the outside walls horizontally across the garret to a large central chimney.

The early huge chimneys had only one flue. It was big enough for a man to crawl through. It served two or three fireplaces on the first floor of a house and often one or two small fireplaces on the second floor. Since the fireplaces did not have dampers, heat was sucked from the rooms up the chimney in enormous volume unless the fireplace openings in the parlor, bedroom and garret were blocked off with fireboards. But the kitchen area was kept reasonably comfortable by the never-extinguished fire in its great fireplace .[11]

The lintel of this fireplace, which was sometimes high enough for an adult woman to step into without stooping, was a gigantic hewn oak timber. Behind it was a wooden lug pole, purposely charred to protect it against heat and flame, from which cooking utensils were suspended on wood trammels. In the back of the fireplace, near one end, was the beehive oven, far more capacious than the oven in a modern range. It was preheated by building in it a fire that raised the temperature to as much as 700 degrees. The smoke curled out of the opening into the fireplace and then up the flue. After the fire was scraped out, the food was set in and the opening was closed with a wood cover while the food was cooked by the heat stored up in the bricks.

Much later, the oven was moved out of the firebox and placed at either side for accessibility. It had a hinged cast-iron door and directly behind this a small flue that led into the main chimney flue.

---

[11] The intensity and duration of the fire are evidenced by the cavity the flames and embers chewed into the lower back wall of the firebox. Even the granite and gneiss in Connecticut fireplaces was cut back as if by a big rodent with diamond-capped teeth.

None of the fireplaces in the earliest houses had mantels. But a shallow cupboard was recessed in the vertically paneled walls next to the parlor and bedroom fireplaces.

Other interior walls were paneled or plastered. In the latter instance, they had chair rails or wainscots.

To compensate for the small windows and to brighten the rooms, plaster walls and paneling were whitewashed, but the framing members were unfinished. The wide oak floor boards were also unfinished. They were kept neat by scrubbing with sand stored for the purpose. To offset this drab decorative treatment, the rooms were made colorful with braided rugs or canvas floorcloths and furniture brightly painted to protect against soiling and scarring of the soft pine of which it was made.

One other decorative feature of houses on Cape Cod was the picket fences around them![1][2] But the home owners may never have thought of these as decorative. Rather, the fences were essential to restricting movement of cattle and preventing drifting sand from piling up around the house — which it did anyway.

In addition to the changes made over the years in Cape Cod houses that have been mentioned, there were others, primarily of an esthetic nature.

As the height of the front and rear walls was increased, a frieze was added and the severe cornice was ornamented with dentils and moldings. Windows acquired cornices and the front door was paneled; the flat casings were replaced by decorative pilasters. Raised paneling and bolection moldings appeared on fireplace walls. Houses built in the late Seventeenth and early Eighteenth Centuries acquired many of the stylistic features of the Federal and Greek Revival architectural styles.

Changes were also made in the standard Cape — if there was such a thing — as it increased its geographic spread. For example, in Connecticut stone was used instead of brick in fireplaces, chimneys and foundations. Dormered gambrel roofs are everywhere. Many small full Capes have only one window on each side of the central doorway. And the second story often slightly overhangs the first at the ends of the house.

But all the changes that occured in the Cape Cod house were minor. About 1850, when the style finally succumbed to the mad passion for Victorian, a Cape Cod house was still instantly recognizable for what it was.

Eighty years went by. During that period some new Capes must have been built; a great many of the old ones were substantially changed — and in the process frequently ruined. Then suddenly the Cape Cod house was reborn. Once a strictly New England house, it became a national house. In 1949 the editors of *Architectural Forum* wrote: "If an architect from Mars were to take a crosscountry jaunt along....U.S. Route 6, starting in lush, semi-tropical California and ending on the sandy, windswept hook of Cape Cod...he would be struck by the persistence, throughout his journey, of one particular building type. From Los Angeles east across the arid plains of Nevada and Utah, up the jagged edge of Colorado's Rocky Mountains, zigzagging through the flat farm lands and middle-towns of Nebraska and Iowa into the suburbs of giant Chicago and Cleveland; across the piney tops of the Allegheny Mountains in Pennsylvania and northern New Jersey to Bear Mountain on the Hudson; through the small industrial towns of Connecticut and Rhode Island and up again into Massachusetts' rolling Berkshire Hills, flattening finally toward the ocean, he would see, over and over again, a small, white, box-like house with a pitched roof and shuttered windows....-

[1][2] In Provincetown, according to Thoreau, "tight board walls" were used instead and these were "often set as close as a foot to the houses".

15

Twentieth Century America's most popular house design, now scattered throughout the entire country, is the Cape Cod Cottage...."

One man can be given credit for making it so. He was Royal Barry Wills, of Melrose, Massachusetts.

When Wills started his architectural practice in Boston in 1925, the ancient New England Colonial houses captured his imagination and held it until his death in 1962. Not even his son, who has taken over his practice, can say whether he was especially partial to two-story Colonials or to Capes — he designed both with equal facility — but when the 1932 depression struck, the Cape became his hallmark. He saw it as the perfect answer to the needs of the time. It was charming, livable, efficient, easily built with stock materials, adaptable to modern living, economical. Anyone could build a 1000-square-foot Cape for somewhere around $4000.

To architects intent on popularizing a modern architectural style, Wills was an anachronism to be disdained. But to the public he was the answer to a prayer. I was building and architectural editor of *House Beautiful* in the late thirties and early forties, and I remember that whenever photographs and plans for a new Wills Cape arrived in the office, the members of the staff groaned good-naturedly, "Oh, my God, another!" But nine times out of ten we ran an article about the house. It was what readers wanted. And anyway, despite the overly large chimneys for which Wills had a penchant, it was a splendid little house in every way.

Wills made the Cape Cod house the house of the 1930s, 1940s and 1950s — perhaps of all time — because he was a skillful architect with a rare feeling for the elements that give the house charm and scale and because he was not backward about promoting his firm. (Few architects are; he just did it better.)

A number of other good architects with an equal feel for the Cape joined Wills in pushing it. The shelter magazines were full of stories about the houses, and even before World War II speculative builders, seeing the handwriting on the wall, began to copy and build them on their own. The results were very pleasant.

But it wasn't until after the war that the Cape really swept the country. And inevitably the design suffered. On the surface the Cape Cod house is such a simple design that almost every builder, every carpenter thought he could copy it without benefit of architectural counsel. But the truth is that the Cape has many subtleties. It is like a tree. The average person looking at a tree sees only its color and shape and pronounces it pretty or ugly accordingly. He does not see the individual leaves, the buds, the fruits, the twigs, the bark, the shape of trunk and branches, the stretch of the limbs and the way they give form to the tree. So with the Cape. The average person does not comprehend the effect of the chimney mass. He thinks those flat board casings would look better if moldings were added. He does not visualize what will happen when the house is raised higher off the ground. Most of all, he does not appreciate the exquisite scale of the house.

This raises a question: Why were ordinary, poorly educated New Englanders of the 1600s and 1700s—carpenters, shipwrights, farmers, fishermen — able to create a masterpiece that most people today can't even copy? I don't know. I have never found an explanation.

All that is certain is that when builders and developers after the war started putting up Cape Cod houses by the thousands, they did not do a very good job. True, they did not destroy the house. That is almost impossible so long as one tries to retain the essence of the house — sets out only to "improve" it a little. *Architectural Forum* quoted Talbot Hamlin, architectural historian, as saying: "Of all the thousand and one awful looking houses that are built for speculation, probably the Cape Cod cottage is the least acutely painful."

What postwar builders did succeed in doing was to work over the Cape Cod house until it reached the point where it lost its appeal, its usefulness, its popularity. Dog breeders did the same thing with the cocker spaniel (along with many other highly popular breeds).

But the Cape Cod house is still being built—sometimes well, sometimes not so well.

Leaving the builders out of it—

Royal Barry Wills and other architects like him changed the Cape Cod house considerably from what it was even in the 1800s. The changes had to be made to adapt the house to modern life.

Windows have been enlarged for illumination and ventilation.

The front door and chimney are not always centered in houses corresponding to the old full Cape.

Dormers have been added to make the second floor fully usable. There are gable dormers in front, and where necessary for space, light and ventilation — in the most successful designs — in back. But many good houses have big shed dormers in back; and while the shed dormer provides much more headroom than any number of gable dormers, it detracts from the beauty of a house.

The multiple windows in the gables have given way to one or two large windows.

Most houses have wings to provide more living space and to garage cars. Some houses stretch from end to end roughly 100 feet. In this respect they differ decidedly from the early Capes that grew — occasionally to almost the same length — toward the back lot line. As on the old Capes, however, the various elements of the wings on the new Capes are in scale with one another and with the main body of the house.

Partly because of the addition of wings, partly because of the need for bathrooms and closets (the former unknown and the latter almost unknown in the past), there is no standard plan for contemporary Cape Cod houses. Room arrangements and sizes vary widely. In fact the houses that Richard Wills and his associates design today are considerably different in plan from those his father designed in the 1930s. This shows up most clearly in the kitchen. Royal Barry Wills' kitchens were tiny because kitchens in his time were strictly utility rooms often used only by a maid. His son's kitchens, on the other hand, are a throwback to the keeping room of the original Capes (but not necessarily with a fireplace).

Yet for all these major changes, the Cape Cod house, when well designed, is still unmistakably a Cape Cod house.

Will there come a time when, like the buggy, it is no longer built? Perhaps. Perhaps not.

Here and there are charming Cape Cod houses in very modern dress.

Some people wonder whether the Cape can ever be adapted to passive solar heating without complete loss of character. Yet in one of his books Wills sketched an ideal solar Cape (although he probably was not even thinking of solar heating).

So who knows where the Cape is headed?

Perhaps we shouldn't care. It has endured and served its purpose well for 300 years more or less. There are not many man-made things in this world about which that can be said.

1690—

JABEZ WILDER

HOUSE,

HINGHAM, MASS.

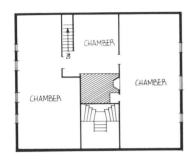

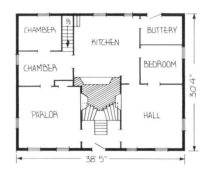

1690—HINGHAM

The Jabez Wilder house is probably the best known of all the many Cape Cod houses. This is not because it's the oldest Cape, nor because it is, as some people say, the first bowed-roof house (it is not). Its fame must be attributable to its unusual beauty. In addition, since it faces the main road into Hingham, south of Boston, it is unusually exposed to view. You can't miss it as you drive by.

These pictures were taken for the Historic American Building Survey in 1936. The house has been little changed since then but during the preceding 250 years it was changed considerably. That should be obvious: Such a sophisticated, finely detailed house was never built in 1690.

The changes made were many. They include the addition of the wing and ell behind the wing; also two bathrooms. Quoins were superimposed on the corners of the house and the doorway was flanked with pilasters. A new kitchen fireplace was built in front of the original huge fireplace. It is possible that the Good Morning stairs were added, because on close examination they look as if they were laid against the paneling. At least some of the paneling also seems to be of later vintage than the basic structure. But the net effect of all these changes has been only to make the house prettier as well as more livable.

PARLOR, ABOVE;   KITCHEN,   BELOW

22

1690—HINGHAM

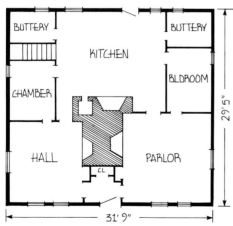

1792—SOUTH ORLEANS, MASS.

The windows in this house are of the size normally used in Capes built in the early 1700s. The openings were approximately 2 feet wide by 3 feet 10 inches high. The panes measured 6 by 8 inches. Although the arrangement of the panes varied to some extent, the upper sash generally had nine; the lower sash, six. The upper sash was fixed; the lower was locked by placing a stick of wood diagonally between it and the top of the frame. Double-hung windows in which both sash slid came later. HABS photo.

24

1746–NICKERSON/GREGORY HOUSE
PROVINCETOWN, MASS.

At the start of the Nineteenth Century, the houses in Provincetown were built on piles so they would not be buried under wind-blown sand. It was a bad idea. In mid-century, when Thoreau toured the Cape, he reported that only a few of the houses were standing and most of them were boarded up. Evidently wind and water got in under them and either carried them away or tumbled them down.

The builders of earlier Provincetown houses understood nature better. The oldest house in town was built tight to the ground and still stands, although it's within a stone's throw of the water. Constructed by Seth Nickerson and preserved for the past many years by John Gregory, it is open to the public and a treasury of information about an enduring architectural style and the way Americans used to live. Only small changes, such as the skylights in the roof, have been made to improve its livability.

One of the most interesting things about the house is that much of the interior—the door frames are a very obvious example—are skewgee. This is not time taking its toll. Early Cape Codders roamed the beaches collecting articles and parts from the innumerable wrecked ships. Nickerson built his house from many of these pieces, which were originally shaped to fit ships' hulls.

EIGHTEENTH CENTURY—WELLFLEET, MASS.

This little half house—only 19 feet across the facade—was, as far as anyone knows, born with its 5-foot-wide wing (which makes it unusual in that new Capes of its era were almost always neat rectangles). The plan follows that of the typical half Cape on page 9 except that the kitchen extends into the wing and has its own small entry in front.

The house, like many on Cape Cod's outer arm, is located far from the center of town and, when built, was as isolated as the HABS picture suggests.

EIGHTEENTH CENTURY—EAST SANDWICH, MASS.

Unless the various owners of this bowed-roof house remodeled it extensively—and there's no evidence that they did—it is good proof that the settlers of the Cape were not always conformists about designing houses. For this is an oddity. The front door is in a tiny wing at the left end of the house (the roof is a continuation of the main roof); and the two closely spaced front windows are placed where the door usually goes. One wonders why a third window was not put in, since there is space for it.

1790—EAST SANDWICH, MASS.

This three-quarter Cape has the projecting windows of the earliest houses but they are sized more like those of later houses and are placed about 8 inches below the cornice (as in many other Capes of this era). There is some thought that the earliest part of the house was the ell (with arch-topped chimney) behind it. The original owners lived in this tiny building until they could get around to building the main body of the house. The garage wing off the ell is quite new and now houses a book store.

1717—LYME, CONN.

In the past five years much work has been done here to correct for the ravages of rot and termites. A small ell was added. But the house is essentially unchanged. It is very similar to the old houses on Cape Cod except that it stands a little higher off the ground and the foundations, fireplaces and chimney are stone. (In this part of Connecticut the stone is striated and easy to work with. Connecticut builders who had access only to field stone, were not so eager to use it because it was much more difficult to fit. Instead, they used bricks.)

1788—WARREN, ME.

In Maine it is standard practice to tie house and barn together so you can get from one to the other without going outdoors in winter. Nevertheless, this full Cape was built to stand alone. The wing came later, probably in bits and pieces, until it reached the barn. HABS photo.

1666—OLD LYME, CONN.

As indicated in a footnote to the main text, the dating of old houses is largely a matter of guesswork and wish-work. That is certainly indicated in this case. Although various owners and country historians have researched the history of the house, there is no solid evidence showing when it was built or by whom. Nevertheless, it seems reasonable to assign the date of 1666 because (1) the house is within a quarter mile of the William Peck house, opposite, and (2) is almost a duplicate of that house (suggesting that, if the two houses were carpenter rather than owner-built, they were probably put up by the same man). Furthermore, this house is situated on an abandoned stage-coach road used in the early days of the Connecticut colony.

1666—WILLIAM PECK HOUSE, OLD LYME, CONN.

The date of the Peck house cannot be authenticated. There's no doubt that it's very old, as evidenced by the framing members. And the ledges at the base of the chimney where it emerges from the roof are a definite indication of antiquity. These are sloping shelves of stone built into the chimney. They were used before metal flashing came into use to guide water away from the joints between chimney and roof.

The house measures 41 feet 3 inches by 23 feet 9 inches and is therefore more of an oblong than most Capes. Accordingly, the two front rooms are somewhat longer than most but about the same depth. The kitchen is 30 by 9 feet. All three rooms have fireplaces. The stairs to the second floor rise from the kitchen parallel to the left end wall.

Unfortunately, a kitchen wing and enclosed porch added in the 1920s do not improve the appearance of the house from the rear. And the house has been remodeled so extensively that many of its original features have been lost or concealed. Even the magnificent oak lintel of the kitchen fireplace has been covered. But in 300 years of occupancy, such changes are almost inevitable.

EIGHTEENTH CENTURY—MADISON, CONN.

This house is so neat and trim that, when you drive by, you're not sure whether it's old or new. Unlike other less well kept-up Capes on the same stretch of road, it bears no date. But it is old, all right. Rarely in a new house does the roof seem to rest directly on the windows. Looking around at the sides, you find that odd tell-tale placement of the gable windows. And upon close examination the paint and wood are a dead giveaway of age.

1783—EAST DENNIS, MASS.

A beautiful three-quarter Cape in a well manicured setting.
It has a frieze, as many houses of this period did not; but
it is broken by the window heads and transom over the
door. The two large and one small window in the gable
are unusual; however, the unusual arrangement of these
windows is never unexpected. As Thoreau noted, second-
story windows in Cape Cod houses seemed to be placed
wherever they suited the occupants of the second floor.

EIGHTEENTH CENTURY—ROCKPORT, MASS.

To some people, these are Cape Ann cottages. But if we gave special names to every variation of every architectural style, confusion would reign. So with all due deference to the Cape Anners, let's identify these tiny houses properly. They are simply half-size Cape Cod houses with gambrel roofs. But it's true that they are rather peculiar to Cape Ann—the stubby peninsula north of Boston that is perhaps best known outside Massachusetts for its famous fishing port, Gloucester.

Just why the early settlers on Cape Ann liked to surmount their half Capes with gambrel roofs is no clearer than why Cape Codders liked bow roofs. Probably they needed gambrels to give them enough living space in such little dwellings. However, there are other half Capes in the area with gable roofs; so one guess is as good as another.

Anyway, they're cute houses; different. And the one above is a favorite of the artists and camera-toting tourists crowding Rockport in the summer.

1700–OLD SAYBROOK, CONN.
Details on following pages.

1700—OLD SAYBROOK, CONN.

Most people who are unfamiliar with old New England probably expect Cape Cod houses to be overlooking the water. They rarely are. A location well back from the water and preferably in the lee of a hill was usually selected. This house, then, is an exception—although only a minor exception because the water it overlooks is a cove. The winds at times are fierce but never so fierce or persistent as those blasting homes directly on Long Island Sound.

The house is a charmer, admirably restored—mainly inside—by its present owners. The bowed-roof dormers are highly unusual.

1700—OLD SAYBROOK, CONN.

It is quite possible that this house was built by the same man who built the gambrel on the preceding pages. They are within a hundred yards or so of each other. This one has gable dormers; otherwise they're almost exactly alike. In the old days, even more than now, it was standard prac-tice for builders to construct the same house over and over again.

The garage wing, of course, is an addition; and the solar panels on its roof are brand new. The owners must be congratulated for putting them there. Many people would have put them on the house roof, thus destroying the beauty of the place.

1678–SACONESSET HOMESTEAD
WEST FALMOUTH, MASS.

As first built, the Saconesset Homestead was a full Cape with bowed roof and a great fireplace/chimney block built of stone (which was unusual on Cape Cod). Later a half house was added to the west end (bottom picture). This, too, has a bowed roof in continuation of the original roof. Still later an ell with gable roof was added on the north side. Other changes included the addition of a projecting vestibule on the east end. This incorporates what is now the front door, although the original front door on the south side remains. Probably at the time the vestibule, which is of Classic Revival design, was built, the elaborate projecting cornice was added to the gable to frame the vestibule more suitably. At the other end of the house, the simple rake treatment was not changed.

The house is open to the public.

EIGHTEENTH CENTURY—NANTUCKET

Considering the close links between Cape Cod and Nantucket, it's surprising that the island does not have more Capes than it does. The probable reason is that Nantucket did not develop as early or rapidly as the Cape, and when it did, it was because of the whaling industry. Whaling made a good many men rich, and rich men were not content with simple little houses.

Another possible reason for the present scarcity of Capes is that they were floated across to Cape Cod. This is definitely known to have happened. But it is unlikely that the number leaving the island was large. Furthermore, it is uncertain whether these were existing houses or houses made expressly for exportation.

Be this as it may, Nantucket Capes were like mainland Capes. Witness these two houses. It's true that each has peculiarities, but they are attributable to the owners rather than the island population as a whole. The house at left has two chimneys, though the end one was probably a late addition. Although the house below has the fenestration of a three-quarter Cape, it's actually a full Cape with one window missing. The roof is a half gambrel; that is, it's a gambrel in front, a gable in back. The shed dormers are late additions. Just visible at the back of the house is a small lean-to addition of a type known as a Beverly jog. HABS photos.

45

1746–EAST DENNIS, MASS.

Here's what we think of when Cape Cod houses are mentioned: a full Cape behind a picket fence. Is there anything more beguiling?

This house lacks the plainness or severity of earlier Capes and even of many of the same period. The door is framed by pilasters given an unusual entasis (although the pilasters on another house shown are similarly treated). Slightly sculptured boards trim the windows. The cornice is dentiled.

1760—LYME, CONN.
Details on following pages.

1760–LYME, CONN.

There is no pat reason why the builders of early Cape Cod houses varied the roof pitch. It may have been that one angle was more pleasing to a particular builder than another. Or houses with lower pitches may have been more exposed to wind. But the most likely reason is that roof pitch was related to second-floor headroom. In a deep house you didn't need so much pitch to provide a reasonable amount of space in which you could stand straight. In a shallow house, on the other hand, you needed a greater pitch to provide walk-around space.

But there are plenty of houses that defy the latter two theories, and this is one of them. On most Capes the roof has a pitch of 8 to 10 inches per horizontal foot. Here the pitch is almost 12 inches. Yet the house is not exposed to severe winds. And it is not unusually shallow. So the builder must simply have liked the effect of the steep roof.

The family that has owned the house for almost 60 years insists that, except for two small additions, the house is very much as they found it. However, changes have been made and they are responsible for some of them. For instance, the paneling around the kitchen fireplace, which measures 5 feet across, is new. The wall around the tiny fireplace on the second floor is also new (there was no wall at all when the present owners arrived). The wall that enclosed the stairs to the second floor was removed. The first-floor ceilings are also new although they date back well into the Nineteenth Century. Originally, the joists were probably exposed. Now the only exposed timbers are the lower halves of the summer beam in the bedroom and the chimney girt in the kitchen.

The corner cupboard and oven to the right of the kitchen fireplace are original.

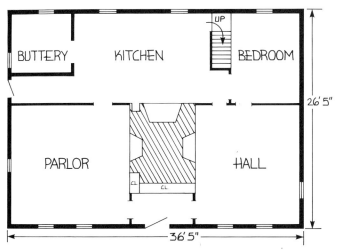

EIGHTEENTH CENTURY—OLD LYME, CONN.

Except for the number of dormers and slight differences in placement, these three gambrel-roof Capes show a marked similarity, and there are many others in Connecticut like them. Compare the roof shapes with those of Massachusetts gambrels. These were designed to give maximum headroom whereas the Massachusetts roofs are often considerably lower.

The house at top left was built in 1710. Even a blind man would have little trouble guessing its age once he had stepped inside because the floors are a roller-coaster. The house at bottom left is dated 1795. That below was built in 1790 and according to its present owners had been badly messed up by inexpert remodelers before they restored it.

PLYMOUTH

MIDDLEBORO

WRENTHAM

EIGHTEENTH CENTURY–MASSACHUSETTS

The differences in roof slopes of gambrel-roof Capes are clearly visible in these three houses, none of which is on Cape Cod. It's interesting also to compare them with the roof slopes of Connecticut houses. Only in the Wrentham house is the lower section of the roof as steeply pitched as in Connecticut.

All three houses have suffered indiginities at the hands of later owners who remodeled them. Fortunately, it takes a lot of maltreatment to destroy the basic character of a Cape. HABS and EAA photos.

1841—BLISS/BOND HOUSE
KAPAAU, HI.

Although New Englanders who migrated to the Western Reserve rarely built Colonial homes (see pages 72-73), the missionaries and whaling captains who went to Hawaii frequently did so. In fact, a number of them had houses prefabricated in New England and shipped around Cape Horn to the islands. There is no explanation for why they, unlike the settlers in the Reserve, felt so strongly about living in the kinds of houses they grew up in; but my guess is that, being so far from home in a totally foreign environment, they just wanted something substantial to remind them of their past. They were also loath at first to try anything else.

Perhaps because ample space was needed for family and compatriots, almost all the early Colonial houses in Hawaii are two stories tall. But several people who should know a Cape Cod house when they see one claim there are also a few of this design. If so, they are very elusive houses. By pure chance, however, I finally found in the Department of Interior files reference to the Bliss/Bond

house. I can understand why no one in the islands called it to my attention: For one thing, it is hidden away on the northern tip of the big island named Hawaii and it is no longer instantly recognizable as a Cape—especially to those unfamiliar with Cape Cod houses.

Although it is generally referred to simply as the Bond House, the original section was built by the Rev. Isaac Bliss, who was born in Warren, Massachusetts, and was graduated from college and theological school in that state. Mr. Bliss was joined soon after he occupied the house in 1841 by the Rev. Elias Bond, from Hallowell, Maine; and in the same year, after Mr. Bliss became ill and returned home, the latter took sole possession of the house. He later enlarged it to pretty much what it is today—a rather shapeless structure 95 feet long and 62 feet deep overall. But Mr. Bliss should get the credit for the basic Cape Cod design, which he understandably altered somewhat to suit the tropical climate and a tropical mode of life. The house he put up ran from the left (west) end of the high

gable roof to just beyond the right dormer—a length of about 48 feet. There were no dormers and the roof, which was thatched, was not so steep as it is now (the rafters of the first roof are still in place). The roof ended at the eaves directly above the front and back walls (the porches around the house were added by Mr. Bond). Because fireplaces were not needed in Hawaii for heating—just for cooking—, the only chimney was in the kitchen wing—the structure attached to the left front corner of the house— and it was destroyed by an earthquake. The fireplace remains. It has a crane, beehive oven on the right side and a wood-storage bin.

The original house is of frame construction straight out of a New England carpenter's book. (By contrast, Mr. Bond's walls in the east wing—just barely visible above— are made of lava.) The framing members are heavy timbers rough-hewn out of a native tree called the ohia. They are fastened together with mortise and tenon joints. Photos by Russ Wilson.

1839–LYMAN MISSION HOUSE, HILO, HI.

Shortly after I pinned down the Bliss/Bond house as a Cape, I heard from Christina Lothian, archivist for the Lyman House Memorial Museum. The old Lyman house, she said, had been a Cape and she sent this daguerreotype print to prove it. But you would never recognize it as a Cape today—and it isn't.

The Rev. David Belden Lyman, the missionary who built the house, was born in New Hartford, Conn., and educated in Massachusetts. The house had a very steep, high thatched roof and no chimney (the kitchen with fireplace was in a semi-detached building at the left end). It was built of wood cut in the nearby forests. The doors, as in the Bliss/Bond house, were koa. The windows were—and still are—glazed with glass brought from New England.

When the house was expanded in 1859 into a two-story structure, the second-floor porch was added (the first-floor porch was probably an earlier addition) and the thatch was replaced by steel.

1796–OLD LYME, CONN.

This house was moved to its present site, given a wing and modest modern conveniences. It's owned by the Lyme Historical Society but is not open to the public. If and when it is, you'll find it as simple and charming inside as out. (though a bit unusual since it is thought to incorporate a still earlier house).

Comparing the house with a New Englander's version of a little grass shack in Hawaii or with the John Stark Edwards house on pages 72-73 or the Greek Revival-treated house on page 103, you may wonder how such houses can be called Capes. But don't we call white and yellow roses roses even though the first rose was probably red-dish? Don't we call today's American cocker spaniels cockers even though they're runts alongside the first cockers?

Houses of any given architectural style change in appearance, plan and size. But as long as they remain basically true to the style, they should carry the name of that style—as do roses and cockers. The Lyman house opposite is no longer a Cape but was originally. By contrast, the Bliss/Bond house, though greatly altered, was and is a Cape. The Edwards and Greek Revival houses were built as you see them (minus the wing on the latter); and if you prefer to call them, respectively, a vernacular house and Greek Revival house, you can, but they are still basically Capes.

EIGHTEENTH CENTURY
EAST DENNIS, MASS.

There was a long bleak period when Cape Cod
houses were allowed to go to rack and ruin.
Some still look pretty seedy. But the current
interest in maintaining and restoring antiquit-
ies is standing them in good stead. This one
is undergoing just minor repairs. Who today
would allow anything as charming to go even
a little bit downhill?

The corniced twelve-over-twelve windows
indicate that the house is not one of the earliest. So does the beautiful doorway (with pilasters like those of the house on page 46).
Fanlights like this came in when height was
added to the front and back walls. In some
cases, the fans were not glazed but filled with
carved wood panels. If the door was shuttered,
as some were, the shutters sometimes had an
arched top that covered the fan.

1735—HANCOCK/CLARK HOUSE, LEXINGTON, MASS. (RIGHT)

Here's a case of the tail wagging the dog. You might think the little gambrel roof Cape was the addition. Actually, it came before the two-story section. It's just one big room with a garret. It has a resemblance to the so-called Cape Ann cottages described on pages 36-37.

The signs saying the house was built in 1698 are inaccurate. There probably was a house on the site then, but not this one. The Cape was built or moved here about 1735.

The house is open to the public from spring to fall. It's a short walk out Hancock Street from Lexington's famous battle green.

EIGHTEENTH CENTURY—SANDWICH, MASS.

Like many old houses on Cape Cod, this half Cape faces the old King's Highway (Route 6a). It's so hidden behind trees and shrubs that drivers skimming by hardly notice it, and if they do, they see only another tiny house. But if you turn down the lane alongside, you fine that it stretches to about twice its original depth—as many Capes do.

In most architectural styles, end chimneys are placed at the very end of the roof and often rise entirely outside the house. In the half Cape, however, the chimney is always set in from the end of the roof a foot or more.

NINETEENTH CENTURY—DUXBURY, MASS.

These two full Capes, dated 1797 (left) and 1802, almost face each other across the street. They are proof that, contrary to some authorities, Cape Cod houses did not always face south although that orientation had much to recommend it: In the two front rooms—parlor and hall—fires were not kept burning, so the more sun heat they received, the better. In the kitchen, on the other hand, the fire never went out; so despite the room's northern exposure, it stayed warm all day and well into the night.

Both houses have projecting vestibules, which the early builders called porches. This is a not uncommon feature of later Capes. The extra space was designed so that coffins could be maneuvered through the tiny entry and out the front door in a horizontal position.

1785—WEST CHATHAM, MASS.

In the early Cape Cod houses the ceilings were only 7 feet high. There were several practical reasons for this: (1) Exterior wall height could be reduced to increase resistance to the winds. (2) The cubage of the rooms was reduced an eighth, thus making them easier to heat. (3) People were, on average, quite a bit smaller than now. But gradually, over the years, ceiling height was raised and with it came a corresponding increase in wall height until it reached a point where there was a foot or more of space between the window heads and eaves—as you see in this half Cape. HABS photo.

1740–CHATHAM, MASS.

Weather takes a toll of old houses, especially along the shore. On Cape Cod and the islands off it, siding must be replaced rather frequently, which accounts for the newness of the shingles here. Before window makers adopted the practice of treating sash and frames with water repellent and preservative, windows were rotted out rapidly by water collecting on the horizontal surfaces. When that happened, the windows had to be replaced and, in the process, the home owners often changed the style of the sash to whatever was then in vogue. This probably explains why the sash here have only two big panes. But Cape Cod houses survive such changes, if not always happily, at least with equanimity. Take away the paved road and power lines and you can visualize the woman of this household in her bonnet waiting anxiously at a window for her husband to come in from fishing.

Compare the chimney with that opposite. Here it's centered over the doorway (the usual practice); there it's at the other end of the house. The latter is also a small chimney for a stove. This one is larger—although a trifle small for a dwelling of its vintage. But note that the base is bigger than the trunk, indicating that it may have been rebuilt when the fireplaces were no longer the only heat source.

1825—TRURO, MASS.

Next to those Cape Cod houses that have been demolished, I don't know of any that have been so maltreated as this one. Imagine a Cape being turned into the Victorian monstrosity at left! But hurrah for the family that came along and returned it to its original appearance.

The slight second-story overhang at the gable ends is very unusual outside Connecticut. HABS photos.

1830—TRURO, MASS.

Though there's reason to think that small Capes—especially half houses—were built to be lengthened, they rarely were. Here is an exception. It started life as a three-quarter Cape. Then in 1940 the right end wall was moved outward and a new section was inserted, with the result that the part to the right of the door is slightly longer than that to left. The wing was added a year later.

The paneling in the old parlor (left of front door) is unusually simple for 1830. Placement of a cupboard beside the fireplace, however, is typical of Capes. HABS photos.

NINETEENTH CENTURY—HALIFAX, MASS.

At the time these pictures were taken in 1935 for the Historic American Building Survey, the trellises (which did not help the appearance of the house) were beginning to collapse. The house had also acquired dormers. But it was a very appealing place and inside it was in good repair. The pilasters of the doorway and the parlor paneling and cupboard are refined. In the kitchen (page 70), the fireplace lintel is made of brick supported by a steel bar rather than the huge oak timber that was typical of much earlier fireplaces. The beehive oven has been moved forward from the back of the fireplace but is still contained within the firebox. The ceilings are plastered, and the hewn chimney girts in the kitchen are the only timbers showing.

HALL

KITCHEN

EIGHTEENTH CENTURY—YARMOUTH, MASS.

The full Cape with only two front windows is quite common in Connecticut, but as this little house proves, it was not unknown on Cape Cod. The roof is so slightly bowed that it is hardly discernible. The only possible purpose of such a minimum curvature was to strengthen the roof.

The white chimney with a black stripe around the top is often seen on houses located on the Cape. In *"A Book of Cape Cod Houses"* (which covers all types of house built on the peninsula through the Victorian era), Doris Doane notes that, while the purpose of the color scheme is uncertain, "it is believed that during the pre-Revolutionary and Revolutionary days chimneys were painted in this manner by those who wished to signal their loyalist sympathies." HABS photo.

1807—JOHN STARK EDWARDS HOUSE, WARREN, OHIO

As the Connecticut Colony was set up by charter from King Charles II in 1662, it ran in a narrow strip from Narragansett Bay to the Pacific Ocean. After the Revolutionary War, the state claimed title to all this land but was finally persuaded by Congress to give it up. It did so, however, only with the proviso that it be allowed to retain a tract that extended 120 miles west from Pennsylvania's western border and from Lake Erie south to 41 degrees north latitude. This tract was known as the Western Reserve of Connecticut, or simply the Western Reserve. Connecticut planned to sell the land to its citizens at a price of six shillings per acre. At the western end of the Reserve, a half million acres were set aside by the state as "Firelands" to be given to state citizens who had been burned out by the British during the war.

That many Connecticut people took advantage of this scheme in the early 1800s, after various Indian problems had been ironed out, is attested by the number of Ohio towns that are named after older towns in Connecticut. Most of these are in Ashtabula, Trumbull and Mahoning Counties, at the eastern end of the Reserve, and in the Firelands counties of Erie and Huron at the western end.

Logically, a good many of the Connecticut families (as well as families from other New England states) that moved to the Western Reserve should have built houses similar to those they had formerly lived in. This was common practice among migrants in the early days of the United States. But the newcomers to the Reserve did not follow this practice.

In the early days of settlement, from about 1800 to 1815, the Western Reserve was a wilderness and the new arrivals were more preoccupied with clearing the land than building comfortable homes. So they made do with log cabins. Later, when the land was under control and more and more people began pouring in, home building got under way in earnest. But by then the Federal style of architecture followed quickly by the Greek Revival style had taken hold throughout the new nation. Consequently, the oldest houses in the Western Reserve are for the most part in these styles.

The John Stark Edwards house is the only Cape Cod house I have found. (There must be others, but where?) Even it is not a very good example of the early Cape. It has two chimneys. The windows have cornices and the front door with sidelights has a matching cornice. The height of the front and back walls has been increased enough to allow for tiny lie-on-the-stomach windows in the second story. Still, the house is an indication that at least some New Englanders loved their Capes so well that they, in effect, took them across country with them. Photo by Hardman.

EIGHTEENTH CENTURY—CLINTON, CONN.

The Cape Cod house opposite faces the green in Clinton. Just up the street is the one above. Beyond this and the two-story Colonial you can just see another Cape. Beyond that is a fourth. All are almost identical. The house above is dated 1725 and the others came into being at about the same time.

On Cape Cod here and there you run into the same thing: One Cape follows another. In one town on the main street three half Capes rise cheek by jowl (alas, I lost my picture of them).

Sometimes today we deplore the sameness of the

houses unimaginative developers threw up in a hurry after
World War II. Well, our ancestors did the same thing, though
not in a hurry. But for some reason that does not seem de-
plorable. Why? Because the Cape has a beauty, a solidity
that no developer has ever matched. In a meadow or wood-
land by itself, a Cape is a one-karat diamond centered on
a piece of black velvet. In a row or a cluster, each Cape
manages to retain its individuality and the group is like a
range of mountain peaks silhouetted against the setting
sun. Would that developers could build Cape Cod houses
as they used to be built. They could cut costs by repeat-
ing the same design over and over again, and everyone
would be delighted.

1765—NORTH DIGHTON, MASS.

Strip off the front porch and you have a Cape Cod house typical of its era. Even so, it would not have much to recommend it. But it has nice interior features. These may seem unusual in such a simple house but are not uncharacteristic of late-1700 and 1800 Capes. HABS photos.

EIGHTEENTH CENTURY
MADISON, CONN.

Driving east from New Haven on the Boston Post Road, you see many old Colonial and Federal houses that bring joy to the heart. Among them are quite a few Capes. This one is rather typical. It's a full Cape, but since it's smaller than the "standard" full Cape, it has only one window on either side of the door. The second story slightly overhangs the first at the ends of the house. Many of the Cape Cod houses in Connecticut have such an overhang. In Massachusetts, however, it is almost never encountered.

1753—MADISON, CONN.

Another house with a second-story overhang. Modern builders often use a horizontal break in a wall surface as an excuse to use one kind of siding on the first floor and a contrasting siding above, but early builders did not do this. Like the house opposite, this one has only one window on either side of the door. In the three-unit gable window, the center sash is a new addition, because as long as heating was a problem, early home owners had no fancy for big expanses of glass. The shed dormer and porch are also obvious additions.

1752—JOSEPH ATWOOD HOUSE, CHATHAM, MASS.

The two wings that have been added to this house since its construction show in the picture but not in the plan (next page). Unfortunately, they do not help the appearance of the house, which, despite the fluted, spear-shaped pilasters adorning the doorway, seems unusually austere. (Part of this austerity, it must be admitted, is attributable to the shingles, which are fairly new and have not yet weathered to a grey.) The windows at this end of the house border on the eccentric.

The interior treatment ranges from the severity of the kitchen to the refinement of the corner cupboard (marred by the jigsaw cutout at the base). The house, which is the headquarters of the Chatham Historical Society, is open to the public. HABS and author's photos.

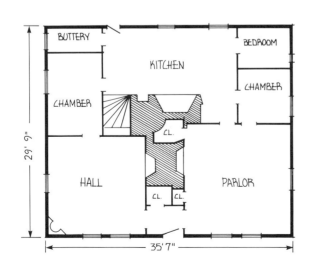

1690–OLD LYME, CONN.

There is something missing here. You've noticed that, of course. The chimney. Its absence is one of those sad things that occasionally afflict ancient houses. When central heating came in, the then owners decided that the three fireplaces and huge central chimney which had warmed the house since its birth were no longer necessary. In fact, they took up much too much space. So out they came (only the enormous foundation is left). They were replaced by a small fireplace in what used to be the kitchen and a miniscule chimney hidden behind the sway-backed ridge.

The house was further spoiled (though perhaps not at the same time) by a big two-story ell, which fortunately is clearly visible only when you come at the house from the north.

Still, it's a lovely old place and its owners, past and present, love it.

At some time in the not-too-distant past this house was moved and flawed by the addition of dormers that are completely out of scale. The present owner, who has done a great deal of restoration work, has considered removing them but has so far been restrained by cost. When he recently resided the house, he graduated the clapboards in the way they were sometimes installed in early days. Those at the base of the walls have an exposure of about 2 inches. This is increased to the normal 4 inch exposure in the higher courses. It has been thought that early New Englanders did this to provide a greater thickness of wood at floor level, thus making the floors warmer. However, since graduated clapboards were used only on the facade (the present owner has used them on other walls, too), the purpose was probably decorative.

The windows project approximately 2 inches beyond the walls as they did in the past. They have no casings.

The stairs are the next thing to a ladder, rising straight up from the tiny front hall to the second floor.

1757—HINGHAM, MASS.

1790—LYME, CONN.

The Cape Cod house's simplicity of line, its
modesty, its affinity with the world make it at
home in every setting—by sea, pond or stream;
perched on a dune on the moors behind the
Cape's Highland Light; in forests everywhere;
on a country road, village green or suburban
street.

Whether ringed with fences or stone walls;
set in a landscaped lawn; shrouded with vines
or climbing roses—it's a lovely home.

And to its owners, whether they're as young
as the couple who live here or in their waning
days, it's a home to be enjoyed and to be quiet-
ly proud of.

1745—GILL, MASS.

Early fireplaces were extremely inefficient and it was not until the Eighteenth Century that they were improved. Most of the credit goes to a Massachusetts native named Benjamin Thompson, better known as Count Rumford. Unlike the cavernous, boxy fireplaces that the colonists copied from their English homes, Rumford's were high and shallow, with a firebox shaped like a truncated V and a back wall that sloped or curved frontward. The effect of this design was to direct more heat into the room and less up the chimney.

The fireplaces in this attractive Cape were designed to Rumford rules. HABS photos.

NINETEENTH CENTURY—TRURO, MASS. (LEFT)

Cape Cod houses almost never are saltboxes because the room under the extended roof would not be high enough to stand in. In this almost-saltbox, however, the room in the added-on ell is usable because the roof is broken slightly upward and the ground slopes away from the back of the house so the floor of the room could be dropped a couple of steps below the main floor.

Note that the owners still follow the ancient practice of painting the clapboards on the facade but leaving the shingles on the other walls to weather. Today, if they paint their homes at all, most people paint all four walls. HABS photo.

1780—OLD LYME, CONN. (ABOVE)

Large ells on old Capes tend to be a motley collection of small buildings joined together. The thing that saves them from looking trashy is that they are all nicely in scale with one another and the house proper. In this case, the ell, added just a few decades ago, was designed with equal care and was put up as a unit. (The big north window indicates that the wing was added for an artist. Old Lyme was once a famous artists' colony.) It adds considerably to the charm of the house, built by a ship captain, although the little roof over the back door is a visual distraction despite serving a worthy purpose. There's a more attractive roof over the front door.

NINETEENTH CENTURY—SOUTH DENNIS, MASS. (ABOVE)

A stark house in a barren setting. But it really isn't so stark as it appears from a distance. The dentiled cornice and fine classical enframement of the doorway indicate an interest in "dressing up" the home—an interest that Cape Codders slowly began to espouse late in the 1700s.

The slender chimney is also a clue to the house's age. (But how much handsomer the house would be with the robust chimney of earlier years.) It indicates that a stove rather than fireplaces was used for heating. EAA photo.

EIGHTEENTH CENTURY—SOUTH YARMOUTH, MASS. (RIGHT)

A charming house in a pretty setting. The chimney is of unusual configuration. The dormers were a later addition. They are well scaled to the house but their formal gables—in contrast to the house's simplicity—give them a vaguely heavy look. EAA photo.

1768—DENNIS, MASS.

Although the left end is concealed by small trees, this is a three-quarter Cape with a sizable addition in back. Note how little the roof projects at the eaves and rakes. The reason probably stems in part from the early builder's sense of scale, his striving for simplicity and his thriftiness (why waste money and time on such non-essentials as wide overhangs?). But the other part of the explanation is that minimum overhangs reduced wind resistance and thus improved a house's chances of withstanding gales.

NINETEENTH CENTURY—TRURO, MASS.

This three-quarter house was brushed by the Federal style of architecture. Witness the fanlight over the door (unfortunately partially reduced in size by an overly tall screen door) and the window cornices. As on the house opposite, the facade is clapboarded; the other walls, shingled; but here the clapboards are not graduated.

The wooden front steps are obviously new and suggest that the sandy soil has been blown away from around the house, because if the sill was originally as high above the ground as it is now, the builder would have installed a stone or brick stoop that would still be in use. HABS photo.

CHATHAM

NINETEENTH CENTURY—MASSACHUSETTS

Even in the earliest and simplest Cape Cod houses the doorways were attractive, and as the years rolled by and the houses became somewhat more sophisticated, they never lost this precious quality. In part this is because the doors themselves were handsome: there is no door so beautiful as the paneled door that succeeded the very early batten doors. But chief credit must go to the treatment of the frame surrounding the doors. Sometimes, it is true, the doorways became too imposing—like those on the opposite page. And the screen and storm doors that have been added in more recent times certainly detract from all doorways. Still, if you get a warm, welcoming feeling as you look at a Cape Cod house, the doorway is in good measure responsible for it. HABS photos.

1835—WELLFLEET

TRURO

97

DIGHTON, MASS.

EIGHTEENTH CENTURY—MASSACHUSETTS

Here are two more "off-Cape" Massachusetts gambrels with differing roof slopes. The comparative youth of the Dighton house is indicated by the cornices over the windows and the fairly elaborate treatment of the rakes. (Don't let the door fool you: it's just a storm door of a kind often seen on old houses.)

The plan of the Lakeville house is somewhat conjectural since the original plan has been lost (if there ever was one). The extensive later additions are not shown. Today the house has a corridor running from the entry to the kitchen and the stairs are parallel to the corridor. This was achieved by demolishing the old chimney and the kitchen and hall fireplaces when central heating was installed. HABS photos.

LAKEVILLE, MASS.

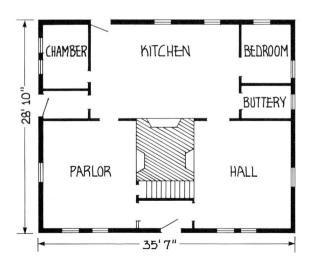

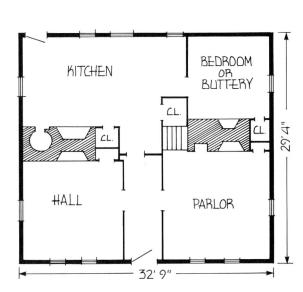

KITCHEN

BEDROOM
OR
BUTTERY

CL.

CL.

CL.

HALL

PARLOR

29' 4"

32' 9"

100

1800–CHATHAM, MASS. (LEFT)

When I asked an elderly waitress how to find the Capt. Solomon Howes house, she drew a blank. So I showed her a drawing. "Oh, you mean the Rainbow House," she exclaimed. "I used to live next door to it. The people who bought it have changed it all around." But in appearance, the house, locally named for its bowed roof, is unchanged.

In some ways, the plan of the original house was better than the usual Cape Cod plan. The center hall wasted floor space but made for better circulation and privacy. There was even space for a pretty good closet. But of course, two chimneys are more expensive to build than one and that must be a reason why other Capes were not laid out in the same way. Early photo by EAA.

1774–SANDWICH, MASS. (ABOVE)

You can't help wondering about the accuracy of the date on this three-quarter Cape when you consider the high clapboarded facade and the very large doorway. They suggest that the house is younger than the plaque on the front states. The big windows also suggest this, but they could just as well have been installed in place of the original windows at a later date—perhaps when other obvious changes were made. For example, the leanto ell is an addition. And either the chimneys have been rebuilt or one of them is a latecomer required for the central heating system. (In either case, why weren't they made the same height and size and of the same material?)

How mysterious old houses can be.

1850—TRURO, MASS. (ABOVE)

In the middle of the Nineteenth Century, many Cape Cod houses acquired a pronounced Greek Revival look. In some cases, as here, the look is so strong that you can hardly call them Capes. The eaves were raised well above the windows. The houses had pilasters, rather monumental doorways, heavy cornices, enframed gables. And they were turned perpendicular to the street, with the entrance in the gable end.

   Finally, the Cape just about disappeared—only to be revived in the 1930s. HABS photo.

NINETEENTH CENTURY—TRURO, MASS. (LEFT)

In the limited space available for stairways in old Cape Cod houses, the stairs had to be incredibly steep and often peculiarly laid out. Here is an unusual example. It makes a tight U-turn that must drive moving men mad. Worse, it's very dangerous because at the bottom of the straight run there is no landing—only a partial winder, then a step at right angles to the run. HABS photo.

A house that is equally attractive in front and back is a rarity. This one had to be, because it faces the road and ocean bay. From the water (above), the house looks like the full Cape that it emulates, while the facade (right) resembles the back of many an old Cape.

Royal Barry Wills Associates deliberately designed and laid out the house in this way, because although it's a year-round dwelling, it is meant primarily for summer living; and in summer, of course, the family spends most of its time at the back of the house. Photos by Haskell.

MODERN—BUZZARDS BAY, MASS.

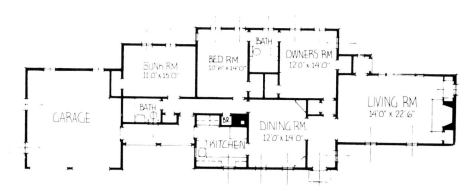

104

MODERN
EAST ORLEANS AND
CHATHAM, MASS.

Cape Cod is no longer a backwater. In summer it is jammed with vacationers and tourists and it has suffered greatly. Like all popular resort areas, it has become in many spots brassy, tawdry, ugly. The inner arm—from the Cape Cod Canal out to the elbow—has changed particularly. The establishment of the National Seashore has done much to save the outer arm, although it crawls with tourists as never before.

But there are still many areas that are essentially preserved. Here many, many houses are being built by retirees and other permanent residents; and in many cases, they are excellent houses of numerous styles. But the Cape Cod house—often much enlarged—continues the favorite. The two splendid examples below overlook the ocean, although

because of their placement, the camera cannot record the fact. The house at bottom left is in Chatham; the slightly smaller one below, in East Orleans. The latter is shingled on three sides and the facade is covered with graduated clapboards.

At top left is the back of another new year round house, also in East Orleans. It is a considerably modified half Cape with wings. Viewed from the rear, it shows what is happening to Capes to adapt them to modern life. Since it faces south and has a lovely panorama of a salt marsh, the dunes behind the ocean beach and, in notches between dunes, the ocean itself, the back wall is in large part glass to bring in both warmth and view. The sliding glass doors in the main body open onto a deck.

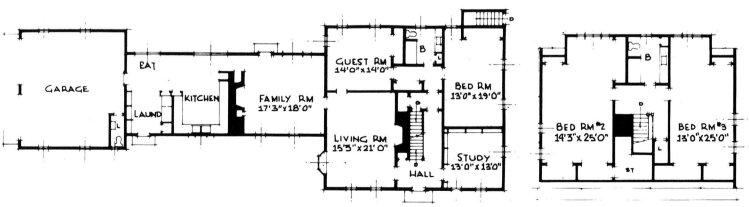

GARAGE

LAUND

L

EAT

KITCHEN

FAMILY RM
17'3"x18'0"

GUEST RM
14'0"x14'0"

B

LIVING RM
15'5"x21'0"

HALL

BED RM
13'0"x19'0"

STUDY
13'0"x13'0"

D

B

BED RM #2
14'3"x25'0"

D

BED RM #3
13'0"x25'0"

ST

L

MODERN—CAPE ELIZABETH, ME. (LEFT)

This Royal Barry Wills Associates Cape has a half gambrel roof (like one of the Nantucket houses on a preceding page). A shed dormer in the gable section helps to brighten and ventilate the long, narrow bedrooms on the second floor but is invisible from the front of the house.

The facade is clapboarded; the other walls, of the compact, almost square main body, shingled. Vertical board siding is used on the kitchen/family room wing for contrast. Photo by Lisanti.

MODERN—SACRAMENTO, CALIF. (BELOW)

In gold rush days, a few of the people who raced to California to make their fortunes followed the missionary practice in Hawaii and had houses prefabricated in New England and shipped around Cape Horn for reassembly in Sacramento and elsewhere. But as far as anyone now knows, those were two-story Colonials and most, if not all, of them have been destroyed. So unless someone can come up with a stray Cape Cod house that followed the same route, this is one of the purest Capes that California has to offer. Of course it lacks a central chimney (the chimney is at the left rear corner of the house) and the windows and doorway are a bit large and there's a shed dormer in back. But otherwise it runs pretty true to form most attractively. Photo by Masterson.

MODERN—NORTH ATTLEBORO, MASS.

Delete the well proportioned dormers and squinch down the windows, and as far as anyone passing by can tell, this is a finely detailed Cape of the Eighteenth Century.

The main part of the house is no larger than an old Cape, but Royal Barry Wills Associates changed the plan to fit modern requirements. This is possible because the fireplaces are not the only source of heat. Other things accounting for the difference in plan are: Our families today are smaller (can you imagine an early American giving up a corner of his house for a porch?). We have more respect for privacy; hence efforts to improve circulation with halls. Photos by Haskell.

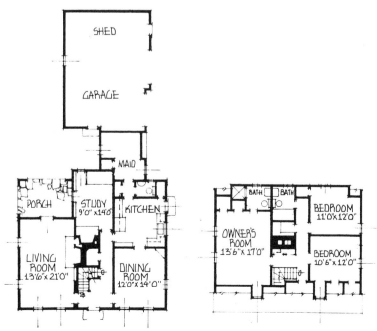

111

MODERN—ROCHESTER, MINN. (ABOVE)

The late Francis H. Underwood was an architect who fell in love with New England Colonial architecture and published a book in the early seventies titled *"The Colonial House Then and Now."* He also designed many Capes and two-story Colonials for his clients in Minnesota and Wisconsin. This is his own house. It has a lower pitched roof than the old houses he emulated because he and his wife had no need for second-story living space. Photo by Breutzman.

MODERN—COSCOB, CONN. (RIGHT)

For many years I lived up the road from this house and knew the architect/owner, Lincoln Hedlander, well. All the neighbors called it a doll's house because that's exactly what it was. Tiny. Exquisite. Until he sold it, Heddy added onto it periodically, but it's still a doll's house.

When Heddy designed it, he aimed to capture the beauty, efficiency and economy of the old Capes; but of course, he planned it for a modern family. It therefore defies the ancient "rules". All you can say about it is that it's a kind of half Cape—very full of charm.

MODERN
EGYPT, MASS.

This house looks larger than it is. The plan explains why. From its hillside perch, the owners can see the sea. In back is an expansive garden. The house is delightful from front or back. Though the rear roofline borders on the eccentric, it is most pleasant—one mark of a good architect, in this case Royal Barry Wills Associates.

In comparison with the exterior, the living room is quite severe but typical of early Capes. Photos by Haskell.

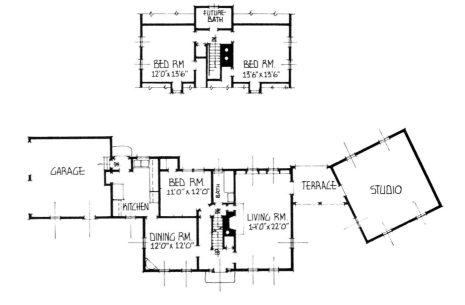

115

MODERN—COSCOB, CONN.

More on next page

Herbert Coggins has not become so famous as a designer of Twentieth Century Cape Cod houses as Royal Barry Wills but ranks with Wills as an architect of rare skill and understanding. This house is probably his best known, having often appeared in print. It is a gem outside and in.

That it strays from early Capes is evident. On the main body of the house, the chimney is centered, the door is not. The house has dormers and wings not only to both sides but also to the rear. Some of the walls are shingled; some are surfaced with flush boards (which were not used until the Greek Revival period).

But no matter. This is a modern Cape at its very best.

MODERN—SANDWICH, MASS.
More on next page

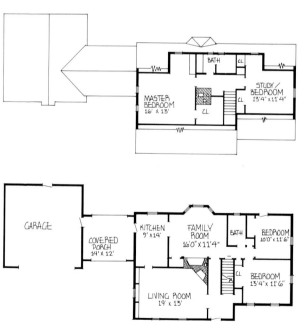

MODERN—SANDWICH

When I first saw this house I was instantly taken by it. It stood well back from the street on a knoll overlooking a pond at the rear. It was obviously new and the owner had taken delight in mounting on the facade a plaque dated 1972—in marked contrast to its next-door neighbor, a saltbox built in 1637.

The house was taken from a design by the late Richard Pollman that had been published and republished in Colonial Homes. The magazine most recently showed the house as it has been built in Durham, North Carolina (the plan of which is shown). The Sandwich house deviates from the plan in that it has a detached garage. And since putting up the house, the owners have enclosed the porch to make a dining room facing the pond.

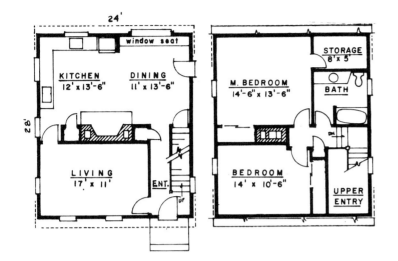

The houses on this and the next two pages are known as Bow Houses. They are the product of Bow Houses, Inc., which provides the plans and an "architectural package" consisting of just about everything that goes into the houses except basic materials such as framing members, masonry materials and kitchen cabinets.

Bow Houses, which have been built from coast to coast—even in the Arizona desert, are a successful compromise between a traditional design and modern living requirements. For example, although the windows are sized to today's needs, the wood sash are glazed with hand] blown 6 by 8-inch panes like those in early Capes. Though the modern floor plan permits only one or two fireplaces, the chimney has the bulk found in early houses. And so on. (Continued on page 123)

HALF CAPE—NOLAN, MD.

FULL CAPE—WEST NEWBURY, MASS.

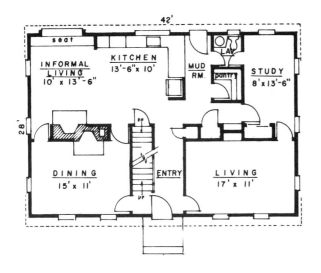

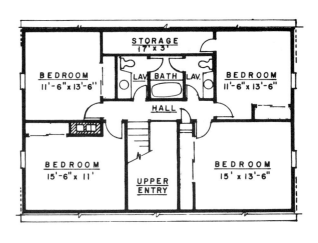

First floor plan:
- seat
- INFORMAL LIVING 10' x 13'-6"
- KITCHEN 13'-6" x 10'
- MUD RM.
- LAV.
- pantry
- STUDY 8' x 13'-6"
- DINING 15' x 11'
- ENTRY
- LIVING 17' x 11'
- 42'
- 28'

Second floor plan:
- STORAGE 17' x 3'
- BEDROOM 11'-6" x 13'-6"
- LAV. BATH LAV.
- BEDROOM 11'-6" x 13'-6"
- HALL
- BEDROOM 15'-6" x 11'
- UPPER ENTRY
- BEDROOM 15' x 13'-6"

THREE-QUARTER CAPE—BOLTON, MASS.

The bowed roofs are supported on 2 by 6-inch laminated rafters spaced, as in most current homes, 16 inches on center. The bow, with a 40-foot radius, is more pronounced than in most of the old bowed-roof Capes. Because of this, the second-story space in which you can stand upright is increased about 20 per cent.

Only one floor plan for each type of house is shown, but there are several variations, and the plans can be varied still more by the addition of wings.

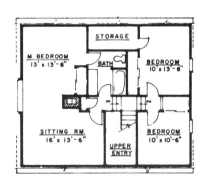

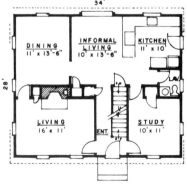

MODERN—OLD LYME, CONN.

In the modern Cape the chimney is as likely to
be off-center as centered; and if dormers are
omitted from the front of the house, there is
likely to be a shed dormer at the rear. This house,
designed by Architect William Thompson, has an
off-center chimney and shed dormer. The latter
complicates the roofline as you look at the side
of the house. But it's a thoroughly charming
place even so.

MODERN—DUXBURY, MASS. (BELOW)

To the eye this house looks much larger than it does to the camera. In
fact, it seemed so extended that, although it is not notable in any particular way, I had to take a picture of it. It's just a nice new Cape—a good
recreation of the old Capes (as it should be in a town brimming with
beautiful ancient houses).

MODERN—MARSHFIELD, MASS. (RIGHT)

Our forefathers avoided exposed locations for their homes for the very
simple reason that they had no way of sealing out the wind and cold.
Despite the energy crisis, we have not to date followed suit—even though
insulation, storm sash and weatherstripping rarely give complete protect-
ion. Perhaps we shouldn't: Light, sun and view are certainly well worth
the few dollars we must pay for extra fuel.

    This is a charming house. From the main body it spreads out in all
directions. It is almost 122 feet long, although the center section is only
42 feet—just a little longer than some of the full Capes built in the 1700s.
Royal Barry Wills Associates were the architects. Photo by Ken Duprey.

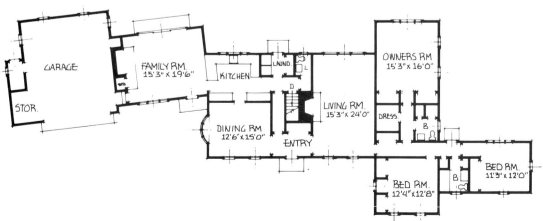

GARAGE

STOR.

FAMILY RM.
15'3" x 19'6"

KITCHEN

LAUND.

L

OWNERS RM.
15'3" x 16'0"

DRESS

B

DINING RM.
12'6" x 15'0"

LIVING RM.
15'3" x 24'0"

ENTRY

D

BED RM.
12'4" x 12'8"

B

BED RM.
11'3" x 12'0"

MODERN—WINCHESTER, MASS.

Royal Barry Wills' own house has all the architectural features that he especially liked in early Colonial homes. The gambrel roof is covered with handsplit shingles; the exterior walls, with graduated antique clapboards. In the study (below) he left the old joists and beams exposed.

The large fireplace is made of used bricks and has an oak lintel. The walls are finished in rough plaster and pine board paneling. Old random-width oak boards are used in the floor. The informality of the room is repeated in other rooms. But the living room, with handsome raised paneling and a fireplace faced with ceramic tiles is more formal. Photos by Lisanti.

MODERN—BROOKLINE, MASS.

About 1950, Life magazine asked Royal Barry Wills Associates—along with six or seven other noted architects—to design a house for it. The resultant publicity was, of course, enormous and the house was constructed by home owners and developers all over the country.

The house shown here happens to be one of the exhib-

ition houses (unfortunately a few of the builder's ideas have been mixed in with the architects'). The original house, which was designed for a family in Minneapolis, served as the prototype. For the magazine, Wills also designed a variation which was actually more faithful to the old Cape Cod style. It did not have dormers and the eaves came down closer to the window heads. Pictures of it are no longer available, however. Photo by Harding.

MODERN—SACRAMENTO, CALIF.

In the building boom after World War II, Californians had
a field day putting up Capes. But a Cape Codder would
not have recognized many of them. This one, however,
doesn't stray much farther off the mark than innumerable
postwar Capes built in New England. To be sure, there are
discrepancies. But why dwell on them? A nice house.
Photo by Masterson.

MODERN—EGYPT, MASS.

Designed for two elderly people by Royal Barry Wills Associates, this house has a lower roof slope than most Capes, in part because the second floor was not expected to be occupied very often. The house corresponds to a half or quarter Cape to which a narrow, deep wing has been added. Because of the breezeway connecting the garage, the house appears larger than it actually is (the first floor has an area of approximately 825 square feet). Photo by Haskell.

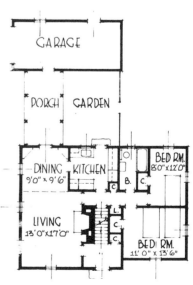

MODERN—HINGHAM, MASS.

Hingham is chockablock with old Cape Cod houses and
the style is obviously cherished there today, because many
new ones are mixed in with the ancients. This one, in fact,
could pass for an old house to which a garage wing facing
the street had been added. Door-length sidelights, however,
were rarely if ever used in the past. In early Capes the sidelights came down to only about the middle of the door
and there were solid panels below.

MODERN—BIRMINGHAM, MICH.

The Detroit area seems to have quite a large number of
Cape Cod houses—all of them of recent vintage, of course.
The two here are among the best, and both would be very
much at home in New England. The house at right is truer
to the basic style: a fine, four-square full Cape. But that
is not to say that the one above is unattractive, because
it certainly is not. However, hidden by the shadows, there
is a break in the facade and roofline just beyond the doorway (the right end is a bit smaller and lower than the left);
and the front windows are very large.

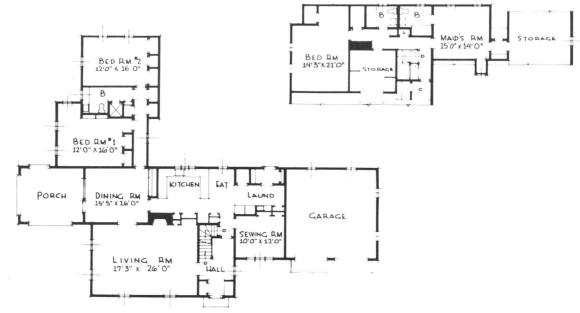

MODERN–SANDWICH, MASS. (ABOVE)

Some Cape Cod houses are remodeled so extensively that they completely lose their identity. This house went the other way. It started life as a run-of-the-mill contemporary ranch house. The current owner, a woodcarver and devotee of Cape Cod houses, decided to turn it into a Cape. Since the plan was that of a modern Cape, only the lines required extensive alteration. The result is a true-to-form Cape Cod house. Its origin is betrayed only by the outside brick chimney.

MODERN–WINCHESTER, MASS. (LEFT)

The half Cape is much less popular today than in the past, but Royal Barry Wills Associates chose the style for this house. This, however, is not a tiny house, and there are many other ways in which it deviates from the original half house. The windows, for instance, are almost twice as large. The chimney, serving a single fireplace and the heating plant, is centered. But the transomed doorway is characteristic of the early Cape Cod houses; and the feel of the house overall is that of an early house. Photo by Lisanti.

MODERN—REVERE, MASS.

This house was built as an exhibition house. Like many of Royal Barry Wills Associates' designs, it has been duplicated by home owners all over the country because it's simple and delightful.

Basically, it's a half Cape with a two-bedroom wing and expansion attic. The first floor has an area of 980 square feet. It was built forty or so years ago when economy of construction was essential. Now that money is tight, the house should be built again. It's far more attractive than today's "contemporaries." Photo by Haskell.

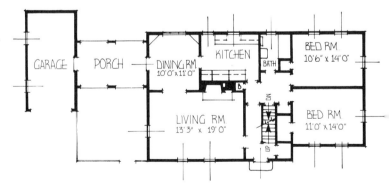

MODERN—PROVIDENCE, R.I.

At first glance, this beautiful little Cape (which turns out to be not so little) looks as if it had been built a couple of hundred years ago. Actually, it was designed only a few decades back by Royal Barry Wills Associates, and this is apparent as you study it more carefully. The central chimney is a little larger and more elaborate than the old ones. The windows are bigger. All walls are clad with graduated clapboards. And the house has gutters; none of the old ones did, although—as an afterthought—sometimes a board was nailed to the roof edge over the door so visitors didn't get drenched while they waited for someone to answer their knock.

Three fireplaces are vented into the main chimney. That in the kitchen, above, is an enormous one with what appears to be a beehive oven but is not. The one in the dining room is smaller but still oversize by modern standards. Both have great oak lintels.

Even in the basement entertainment room the architects took pains to employ details typical of those found in early houses. The shelf with off-center bracket is an example. The dog-leg stairs in the entry are more typical of two-story seventeenth century Colonial houses but not unknown in Capes. Photos by Emelie Danielson.

More on following page.

MODERN—PROVIDENCE, R.I.

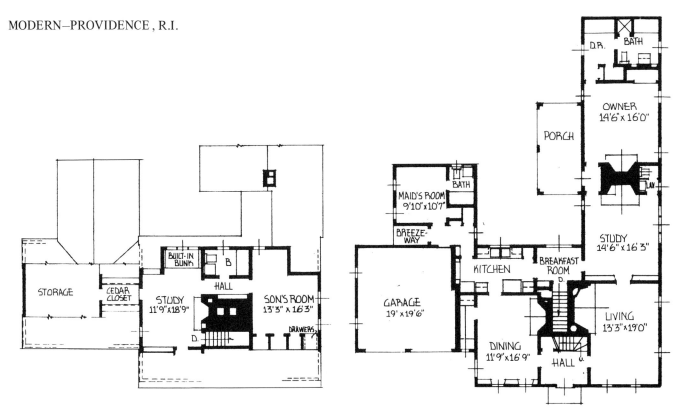

INDEX

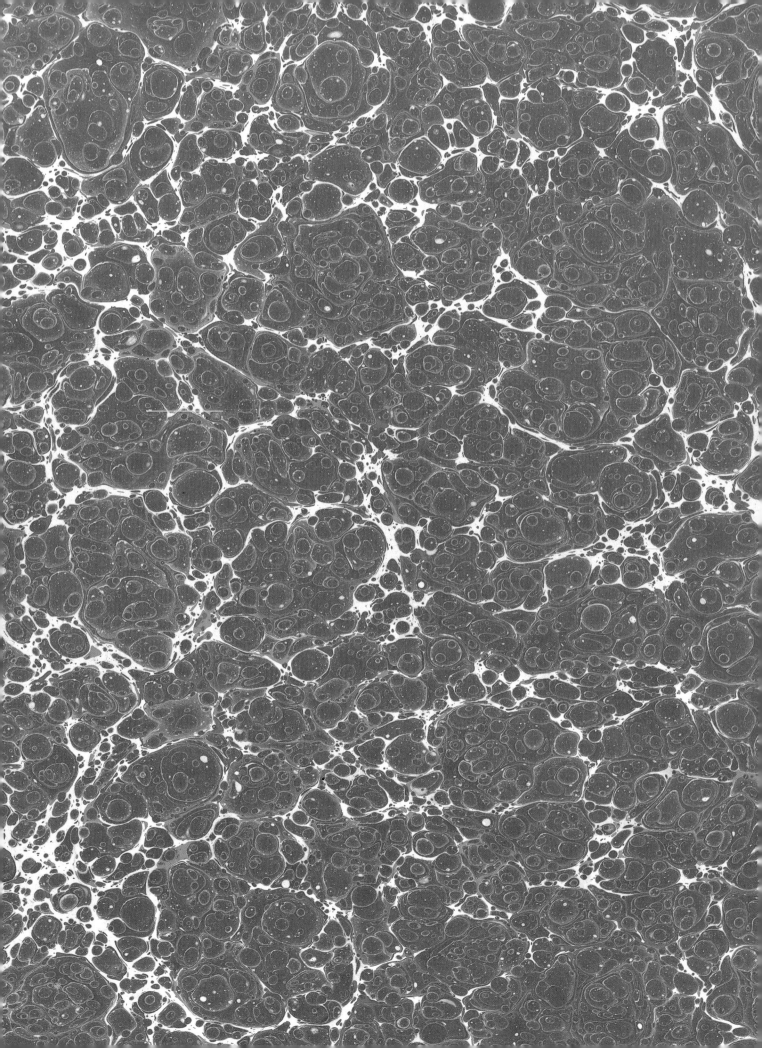